TO:_____

_____

FROM:_____

_____

I Will Not Be Afraid

By Michelle Medlock Adams

Illustrated by Jeremy Tugeau

CONCORDIA PUBLISHING HOUSE • SAINT LOUIS

Published 2017 by Concordia Publishing House
3558 S. Jefferson Avenue, St. Louis, MO 63118–3968
1-800-325-3040 · www.cph.org

Manufactured in USA, East Peoria, IL/063692/412656

1 2 3 4 5 6 7 8 9 10   26 25 24 23 22 21 20 19 18 17

For my brother, Rob,
the bravest big brother a girl ever had.
I love you!

Your kid sister,
Michelle "Missy" Medlock Adams

For Memom and Popup

J.T.

When the thunder booms—KABOOM!
and when the lightning strikes,
I will not be afraid at all!
I won't yell, "EEK!" or "YIKES!"

✤ [Jesus said,] "Why are you afraid,
O you of little faith?"
Matthew 8:26

And when it's really dark at night
and I'm alone in bed,
I will not be afraid at all!
I will not hide my head.

❖ You are a hiding place for me;
You preserve me from trouble; You
surround me with shouts of deliverance.
Psalm 32:7

And when I meet new boys and girls

and I am feeling shy,

I will not be afraid at all.

I will not scream or cry.

✤ Therefore do not be anxious.
Matthew 6:34

And when I have to go on stage
to sing my special part,
I will not be afraid at all!
I'll sing with all my heart!

✤ Shout for joy in the LORD, O you
righteous! Praise befits the upright.
Psalm 33:1

And if our country is at war
and trouble's everywhere,
I will not be afraid at all
'cause I know God is there.

✤ [God] has said, "I will never leave you
nor forsake you." So we can confidently say,
"The Lord is my helper; I will not fear."
Hebrews 13:5–6

I do not have to be afraid
    when bad things come my way.
I will not be afraid at all!
    That's what I have to say!

My God is in control of all—
    the storms, the night, the war.
I trust God and love Him so.
    He loves me even more!

❖ Casting all your anxieties on Him,
because He cares for you.
1 Peter 5:7

God is bigger than anything,
lots bigger than my fears,
And I can call on Him for help,
'cause when I pray, He hears!

✤ "Because he holds fast to Me in love,"
[says the Lord,] "I will deliver him; I will
protect him, because he knows My name.
When he calls to Me, I will answer him;
I will be with him in trouble; I will rescue
him and honor him."
Psalm 91:14–15

God made me to be brave and strong.

But even when I'm not,

God helps me not to be afraid

'cause He loves me a lot!

✤ I can do all things through Him
who strengthens me.
Philippians 4:13

God promises to never leave.

He's always here with me.

That's why I will not be afraid.

I have no need to be!

✤ For He will command
His angels concerning you
to guard you in all your ways.
Psalm 91:11

God sent His Son to die for me.
That sure is great to know!
'Cause even when my life is through,
I know just where I'll go.

I'll go to heaven up above—
and there's no fear up there.
I'll live forever with my Lord,
forever in His care.

✥ For God gave us a spirit not of fear
but of power and love and self-control.
2 Timothy 1:7

'Til then I'll say, "Lord, take my sins,
protect me every day.
Thank You so much for loving me
and hearing when I pray!

"I will not be afraid at all
because You are my Friend.
Your perfect love removes my fear,
and Your love has no end."

✤ Have I not commanded you? Be strong
and courageous. Do not be frightened,
and do not be dismayed, for the LORD
your God is with you wherever you go.
Joshua 1:9

PARENTING MOMENT

The Bible says we do not have a spirit of fear, so do not be afraid! The Bible also tells us that God will never leave us, so we are never alone! Isn't that good to know? Talk with your child about fears of all kinds and about ways to combat those fears. Together, write a prayer that will help to alleviate these fears and instill confidence in the protection and promises that are ours through Christ. This prayer can be as simple as this:

"Jesus, I know You are here with me, and I will not be afraid."

Then, the next time something happens to frighten your child, you can remind him that he is always in God's care and grace.

About the author

Michelle Medlock Adams
is a journalist and author, earning top
honors from the Associated Press, the
Society of Professional Journalists, and
the Hoosier State Press Association.

Author of 22 children's books and 11
books for women, Michelle has also
written thousands of articles for news-
papers, Web sites, and magazines.
When not writing, Michelle enjoys
teaching at writers' conferences and
universities and speaking at women's
events, churches, and youth camps.

Michelle and her husband, Jeff, have
two daughters, Abby and Ally, and
three miniature long-haired dachshunds.
The Adams family resides in southern
Indiana, where they enjoy cheering
on the Indiana University sports teams.

About the illustrator

Jeremy Tugeau received a BFA in illustration from Syracuse University. Primarily a painter, he has illustrated a number of educational early readers and children's trade books.

After spending many years in Nantucket, Massachusetts, and Albuquerque, New Mexico, he and his wife, Nicole, moved to Cleveland Heights, Ohio, with their three children, Ruby, George, and Harrison. They are co-owners of Tugeau2 Inc., an agency that represents artists.